UKULELE
POP HITS
WITH JUST THREE CHORDS

ISBN 978-1-5400-0572-4

HAL•LEONARD®

7777 W. BLUEMOUND RD. P.O. BOX 13819 MILWAUKEE, WI 53213

Visit Hal Leonard Online at
www.halleonard.com

CONTENTS

All About That Bass

Words and Music by Kevin Kadish and Meghan Trainor

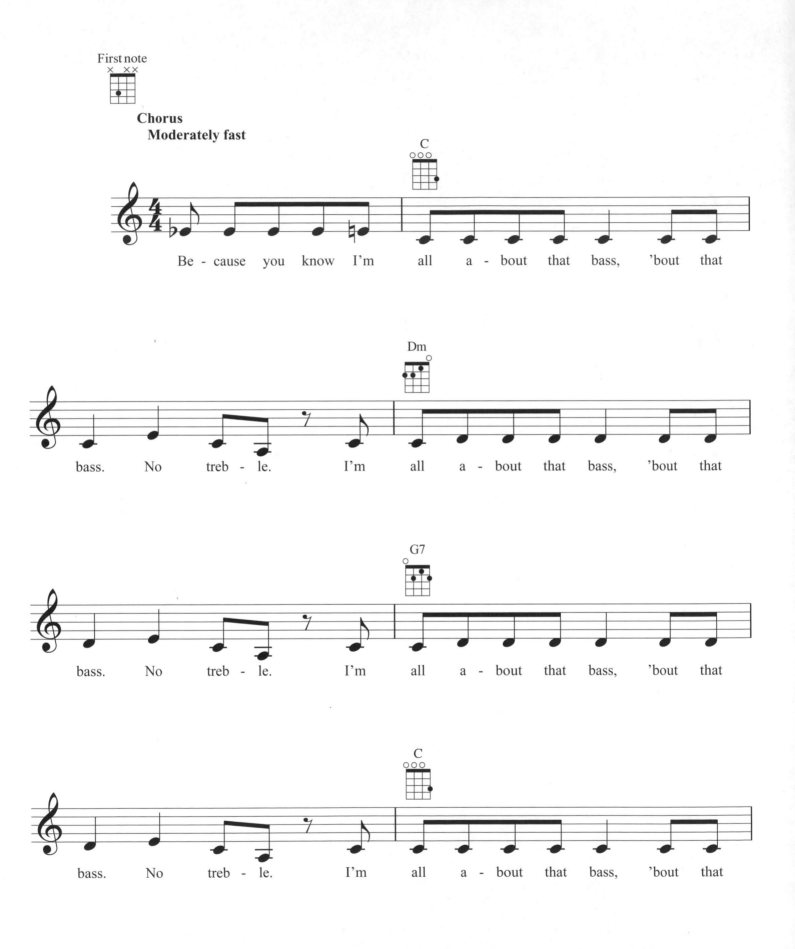

work - in' that Pho - to - shop. __ We know that sh** ain't __ real. __

__ C' - mon now, make it stop. If you got beau - ty, beau - ty,

just raise 'em up 'cause ev - 'ry inch of you is per - fect from the

Pre-Chorus

bot - tom to the top. Yeah, my ma - ma, __ she told me, __ "Don't

wor - ry __ a - bout your size." __

She says, "Boys like __ a lit - tle __ more

boo - ty _____ to hold at night." _____

You know I won't be _____ no stick fig - ure,

sil - i - cone Bar - bie doll. _____ So, if

that's what _ you're in - to, _____ then go a - head _____ and move a - long. _

_____ Be - cause you know I'm

Chorus

all a - bout that bass, 'bout that bass. No treb - le. I'm

all a - bout that bass, 'bout that bass. No treb - le. I'm

all a - bout that bass, 'bout that bass. No treb - le. I'm

To Coda

all a - bout that bass, 'bout that bass, hey. 2. I'm bring - in'

Verse

boo - ty back. _____ Go a - head and tell them skin - ny

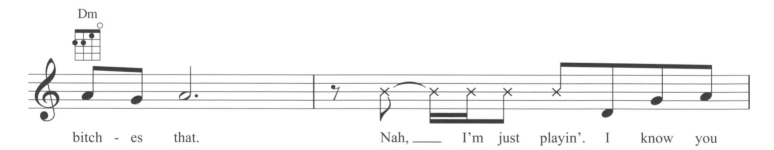

bitch - es that. Nah, ____ I'm just playin'. I know you

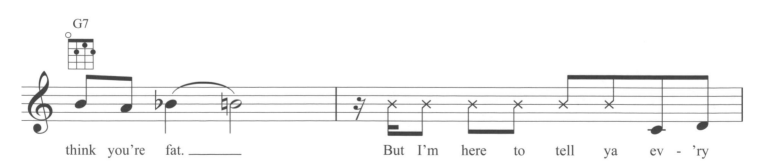

think you're fat. _____ But I'm here to tell ya ev - 'ry

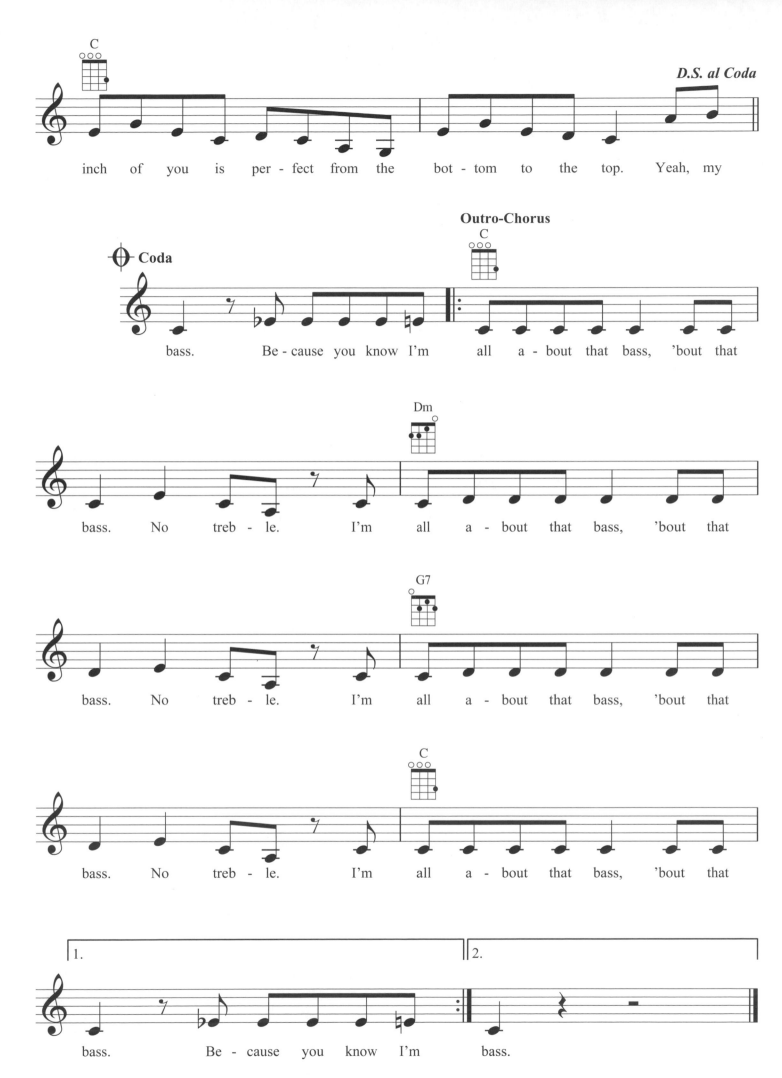

D.S. al Coda

C

inch of you is per-fect from the bot-tom to the top. Yeah, my

Coda

Outro-Chorus

C

bass. Be-cause you know I'm all a-bout that bass, 'bout that

Dm

bass. No treb-le. I'm all a-bout that bass, 'bout that

G7

bass. No treb-le. I'm all a-bout that bass, 'bout that

C

bass. No treb-le. I'm all a-bout that bass, 'bout that

1.

2.

bass. Be-cause you know I'm bass.

Beat It

Words and Music by Michael Jackson

First note

Verse
Moderately fast

1. They told him, "Don't you ev - er come a - round here. Don't
2.–4. *See additional lyrics*

wan - na see your face; you bet - ter dis - ap - pear." The

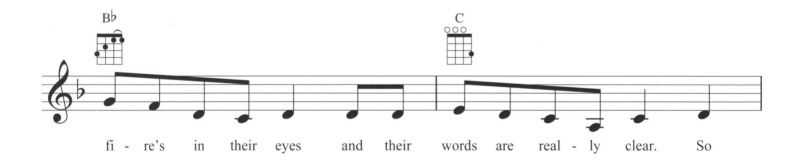

fi - re's in their eyes and their words are real - ly clear. So

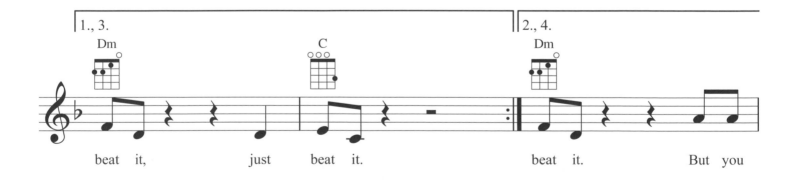

1., 3.
beat it, just beat it.

2., 4.
beat it. But you

⊕ Coda

Outro-Chorus

beat it,   beat it.   No —

—— one wants to be de-feat-ed.   Show-

-in' how funk-y and strong —— is your fight.   It ——

Repeat and fade

—— does-n't mat-ter who's —— wrong or right.   Just

Additional Lyrics

2. You better run, you better do what you can.
   Don't wanna see no blood; don't be a macho man.
   You wanna be tough; better do what you can.
   So beat it. But you wanna be bad.

3. They're out to get you; better leave while you can.
   Don't wanna be a boy; you wanna be a man.
   You wanna stay alive; better do what you can.
   So beat it, just beat it.

4. You have to show them that you're really not scared.
   You're playin' with your life; this ain't no truth or dare.
   They'll kick you, then they'll beat you, then they'll tell you it's fair.
   So beat it. But you wanna be bad.

Closer to Free

Words and Music by Sam Llanas and Kurt Neumann

Verse

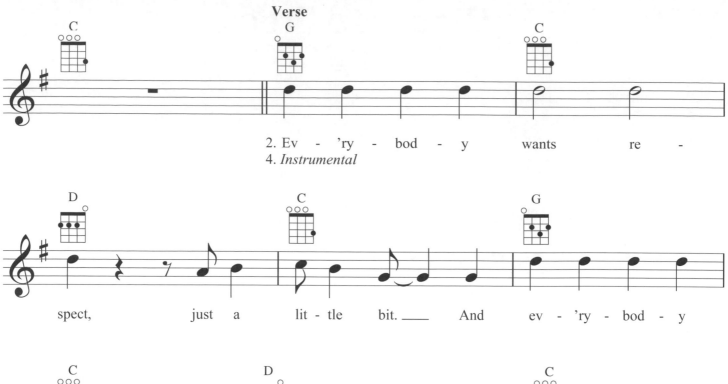

2. Ev - 'ry - bod - y wants re -
4. *Instrumental*

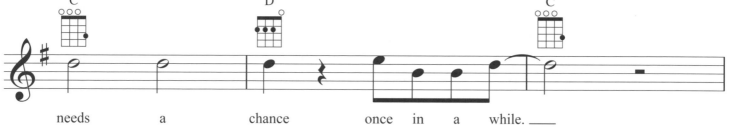

spect, just a lit - tle bit. ___ And ev - 'ry - bod - y

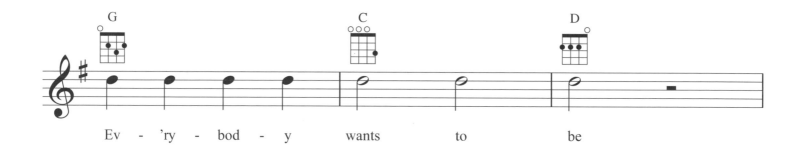

needs a chance once in a while. ___

Ev - 'ry - bod - y wants to be

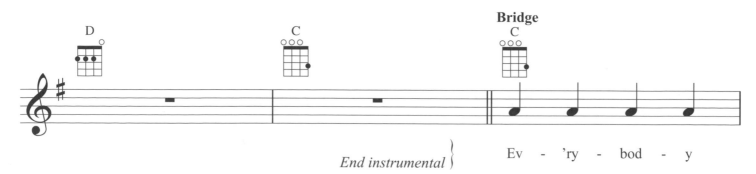

clos - er ___ to ___ free.

Bridge

End instrumental Ev - 'ry - bod - y

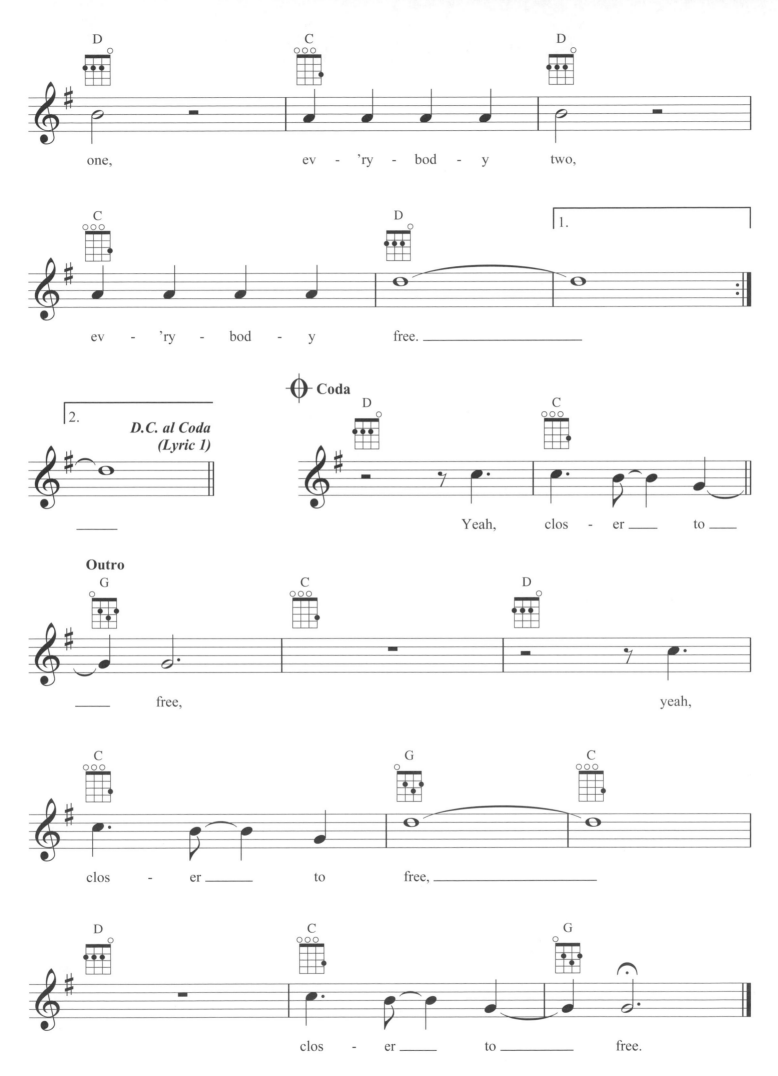

one,   ev - 'ry - bod - y   two,

ev - 'ry - bod - y   free.

1.

2.

D.C. al Coda
(Lyric 1)

Coda

Yeah,   clos - er ___ to ___

Outro

___ free,   yeah,

clos - er ___ to   free,

clos - er ___ to ___   free.

Breakfast at Tiffany's

Words and Music by Todd Pipes

Budapest

Words and Music by George Barnett and Joel Pott

First note

Verse
Moderately fast

1. My house in Bu - da - pest; my, ____ my hid - den treas - ure chest; __

gold - en grand pi - an - o; ____ my beau - ti - ful cas - til - lo: you, ooh, __

you, ooh, __ I'd leave it all.

Verse

2. My a - cres of a land __ I have a - chieved,
3. My man - y ar - ti - facts, __ the list goes on.
4. My friends and fam - i - ly, __ they don't un - der - stand;

it may be hard for you to _____ stop and be - lieve. _ But for
If you just say the words, I, _____ I'll up and run. _ Oh, to
they feel they'll lose so much if _____ you take my hand. _ But for

Bb **F**

you, ooh, _ you, ooh, _ I'd leave it all. Oh, for
you, ooh, _ you, ooh, _ I'd leave it all. Oh, to
you, ooh, _ you, ooh, _ I'd lose it all. Oh, for

Bb **F**

you, ooh, _ you, ooh, _ I'd leave it all.
you, ooh, _ you, ooh, _ I'd leave it all.
you, ooh, _ you, ooh, _ I'd lose it all.

Chorus

C **Bb**

Give me one good rea - son why I _____ should nev - er make a change. _

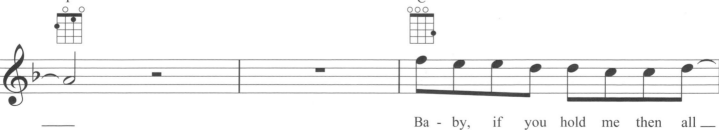

F **C**

____ Ba - by, if you hold me then all _

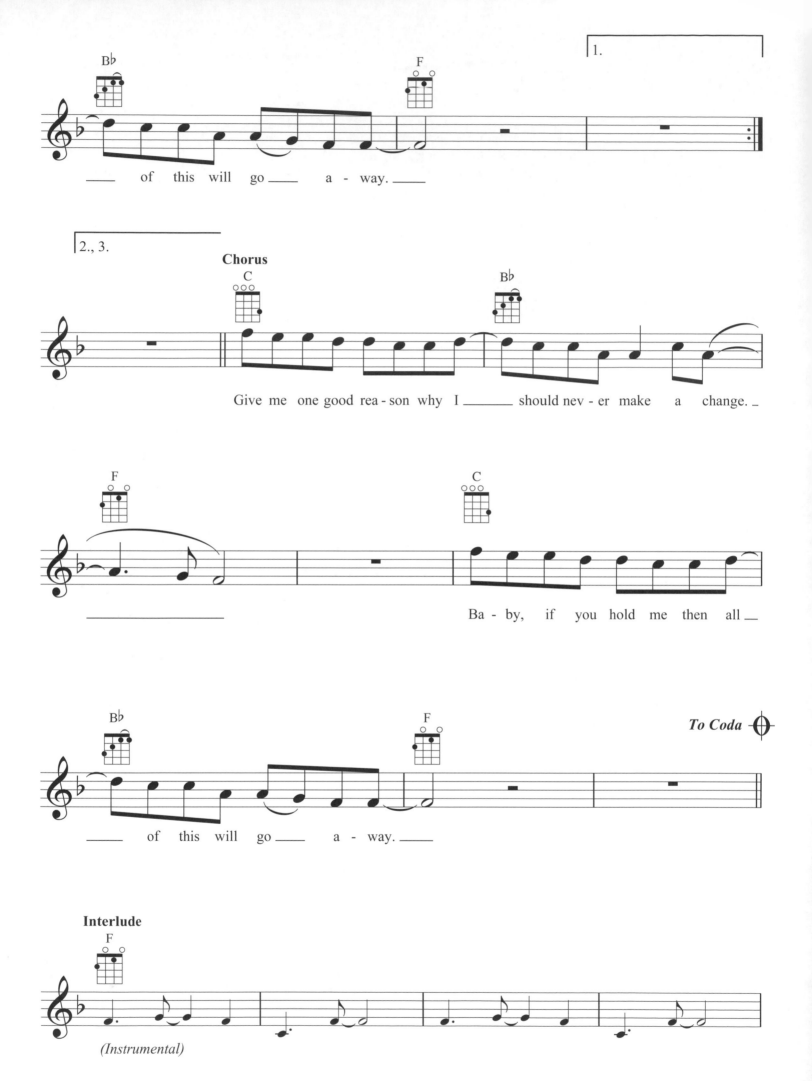

Bb

1.

____ of this will go ____ a - way. ____

2., 3.

Chorus

C   Bb

Give me one good rea - son why I _____ should nev - er make   a   change. _

F   C

_____   Ba - by,   if   you   hold   me   then   all __

Bb   F   *To Coda* ⊕

____ of this will go ____ a - way. ____

Interlude

F

(Instrumental)

Can't Feel My Face

**Words and Music by Abel Tesfaye, Max Martin,
Savan Kotecha, Peter Svensson and Ali Payami**

Pre-Chorus

wor - ry   a - bout ___ it."   She told me, "Don't wor - ry   no more." _

___   We both know we   can't _ go   with-out ___ it.   She told   me, "You'll

nev - er   be a - lone."   Oh,   oh.   Ooh!

D.S. al Coda
(take 2nd ending)

⊕ Coda

Outro

___ it.   Oh. ___

Hey!

Chasing Cars

Words and Music by Gary Lightbody, Tom Simpson, Paul Wilson, Jonathan Quinn and Nathan Connolly

or an - y - one. _____
then not ___ e - nough. _____
to find ___ my ___ own. _____

Chorus

If I lay here, if I just

lay here, ___ would you lie with me ___ and

|1. |2., 3.

just for - get the world?

Bridge 1

For - get what we're told before we get

27

too old. ____ Show me a gar - den ____ that's

To Coda

D.C. al Coda
(take 2nd ending)

burst - ing in - to life.

Coda   **Bridge 2**

All that I am,   all that I

ev - er was ____   is here in your per - fect ____ eyes,

they're all I can see.   I don't know

Outro-Chorus

29

Heart Shaped Box

Words and Music by Kurt Cobain

Chorus

I wish I could eat ___
Throw ___ down your um - bil -

___ your can - cer when ___ you ___ turn black. ___
- i - cal noose ___ so I can ___ climb ___ right back. ___

Hey! ___   Wait! ___

I got a new com - plaint. For - ev - er in debt ___

___ to your price - less ad - vice. ___ Hey! ___   Wait! ___

I got a new com - plaint. For - ev - er in debt ___

to your price - less ad - vice. ____ Hey! ___ Wait! ___

I got a new com - plaint. For - ev - er in debt ___

to your price - less ad - vice, ____ your ad - vice. _

your ad - vice, ___

Outro

your ad - vice, _____

your ad - vice. ____ *(Instrumental)*

Daughter

Words by Eddie Vedder
Music by Eddie Vedder, Stone Gossard, Jeff Ament, Mike McCready and Dave Abbruzzese

Pre-Chorus

Chorus

Hold My Hand

Words and Music by Darius Carlos Rucker, Everett Dean Felber, Mark William Bryan and James George Sonefeld

I wan-na love you _____ the best that, the best that I can. _

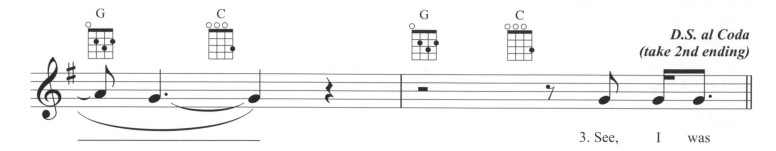

_____

3. See, I was

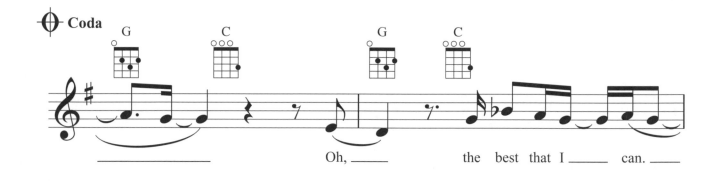

Oh, _____ the best that I _____ can. _____

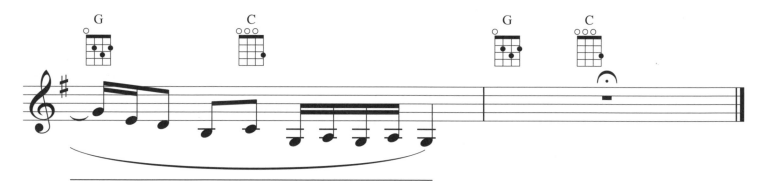

_____

Additional Lyrics

2. Yesterday I saw you standing there.
   Your head was down, your eyes were red,
   No comb had touched your hair.
   I said, "Get up and let me see you smile.
   We'll take a walk together.
   Walk the road awhile."

3. See, I was wasted, and I was wasting time
   'Til I thought about your problems,
   I thought about your crime.
   Then I stood up and I screamed aloud,
   "I don't wanna be part of your problems,
   Don't wanna be part of your crowd."

Just the Way You Are

Words and Music by Bruno Mars, Ari Levine, Philip Lawrence, Khari Cain and Khalil Walton

And it's so, __ it's so __ sad to think that she __ don't see __ what I __ see.

But ev-'ry time __ she asks __ me, "Do __ I look __ o - kay?" __ I __ say: __

Chorus

__ When I see your face, _____

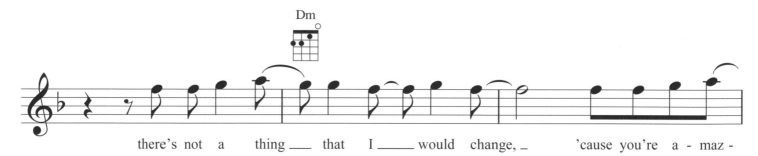

there's not a thing __ that I _____ would change, __ 'cause you're a - maz -

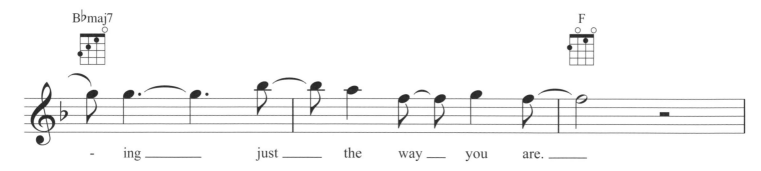

- ing _____ just _____ the way __ you are. _____

And when you smile, __ the whole world stops __

per - fect's what you're search - in' for then just stay the same. __ So __

__ don't e - ven both - er ask - in' if __ you look __ o - kay. __ You know I'll

D.S. al Coda

say: __ When I see your face, __

Bridge

Coda

The way __ you are, __

the way __ you are. __ Girl, you're a - maz -

- ing __ just __ the way __ you are. __

When I see your face, _____ there's not a thing _____

_____ that I _____ would change, _____ 'cause you're a - maz - ing just _____

_____ the way _____ you are. _____ And when you smile, _____

_____ the whole world stops _____ and stares _____ for a while, _____

_____ 'cause, girl, you're a - maz - ing _____ just _____

_____ the way _____ you are. _____ Yeah. _____

I Gotta Feeling

Words and Music by Will Adams, Allan Pineda, Jaime Gomez,
Stacy Ferguson, David Guetta and Frederic Riesterer

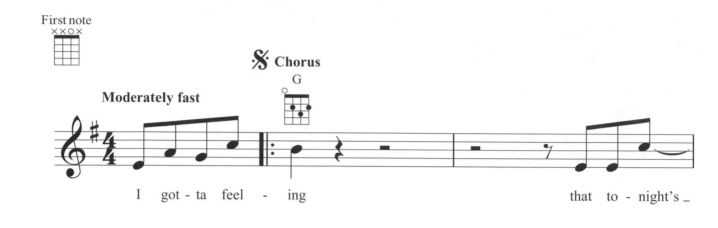

Look at her danc-ing;   just take it   off.   Let's paint the town.

We'll shut it down.   Let's burn the roof   and then we'll do it a - gain. __

Pre-Chorus

_____ Let's do it,   let's do it,   let's do it, let's do

it, __ and do it,   and   do it. Let's live it up, and   do it,   and do it,   and

do it, do it, do it.   Let's   do it.   Let's do it.   Let's

D.S. al Coda
(with repeat)

do it,   'cause I got-ta feel -

⊕ Coda

(Woo   hoo.)

Kiss

Words and Music by Prince

I'm gon - na show U what it's all a - bout. ____
We could have a good time.

U don't have 2 be ____ rich 2 be my girl. ____ U don't have 2 be cool ____ 2 rule my world. ____

____ Ain't no par - ti - cu - lar sign ____ I'm more com - pat - i - ble with. ____

____ I just want your ____ ex - tra time ____ and your

kiss. ____

1.
2. U got to not talk

2.
3. Wom - en, not ____

I Still Haven't Found What I'm Looking For

Words and Music by U2

1. I have climbed _ high-est moun-tain, I have
   (2., 3.) See additional lyrics

run _ through the fields on-ly to be with _ you, _

_ on-ly to be with _ you. _ I have

run, _ I have crawled, I have scaled _ these cit-

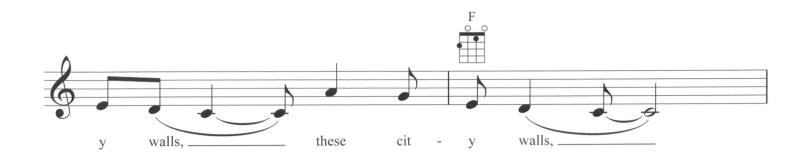

y walls, _____ these cit - y walls, _____

on - ly to be with ___ you. _____ But I still ___

Chorus

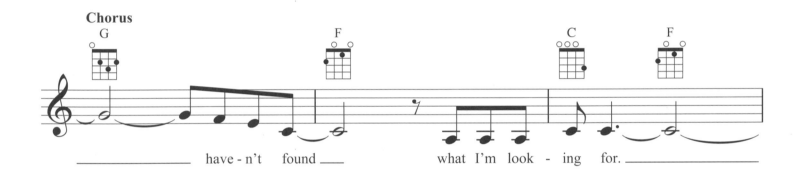

_____ have - n't found ___ what I'm look - ing for. _____

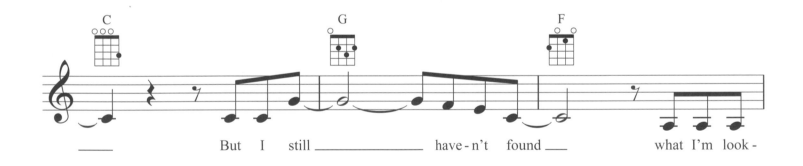

_____ But I still _____ have - n't found ___ what I'm look -

ing for. _____ 2. I have ___ But I still ___
3. I be -

Outro-Chorus

have - n't found _____ what I'm look -

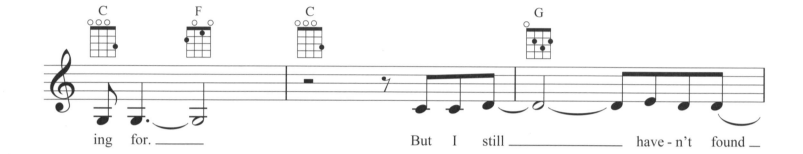

ing for. _____ But I still _____ have - n't found _

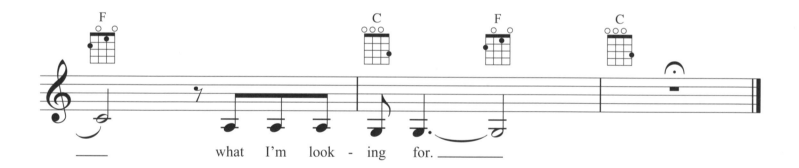

_____ what I'm look - ing for. _____

Additional Lyrics

2. I have kissed honey lips, felt the healing fingertips.
   It burned like fire, this burning desire.
   I have spoke with the tongue of angels, I have held the hand of the devil.
   It was warm in the night, I was cold as a stone.

3. I believe in the kingdom come, then all the colors will bleed into one,
   Bleed into one. But, yes, I'm still runnin'.
   You broke the bonds and you loosed the chains, carried the cross of my shame,
   Of my shame. You know I believe it.

Royals

Words and Music by Ella Yelich-O'Connor and Joel Little

blood stains, ball gowns, trash- in' the ho - tel room. We don't care, __ we're driv- in'

Cad-il-lacs in our dreams. __ But ev-'ry-bod-y's like: Cris- tal, May-bach, dia-monds on your time- piece,

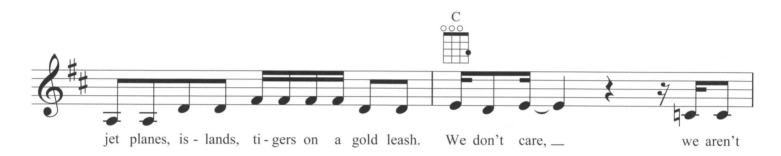

jet planes, is - lands, ti - gers on a gold leash. We don't care, __ we aren't

𝄋 Chorus

caught up in your love af - fair. __ And we'll nev - er be roy - als, (roy - als.)

It don't run in our __ blood. __ That kind of luxe just ain't __ for us. __ We crave a

dif - f'rent kind __ of buzz. __ Let me be __ your rul - er, (rul - er.)

Sad Songs

(Say So Much)

Words and Music by Elton John and Bernie Taupin

And it's times _____ like these _____ when we all _____
The kick in - side _____ is in _____ the _____ line _____

_____ need _____ to hear _____ the ra - di - o, _____
_____ that fi - nal - ly gets _____ to you. _____

And it 'cause from the lips _____ of _____ some _____ old sing -
feels so good to hurt _____ so bad _____

- er we can share the trou - bles we al - read - y know.
and suf - fer just e - nough to sing _____ the blues. _____

𝄋 Chorus

Turn 'em on, _____ turn 'em on, _____ turn on those

sad songs. _ When all hope is gone, _____ why don't you

57

tune   in and turn __ them on? ____   They reach in - to your

room,   oh, _____ just feel __ their __ gen - tle touch. __

To Coda ⊕

When all hope is   gone, ___   a sad song __ says __ so much. __

1.

___   2. If some - one else is   ___

Bridge

Sad   songs, __ they __   say,   sad   songs, __ they __

say.   Sad   songs, __ they __   say,

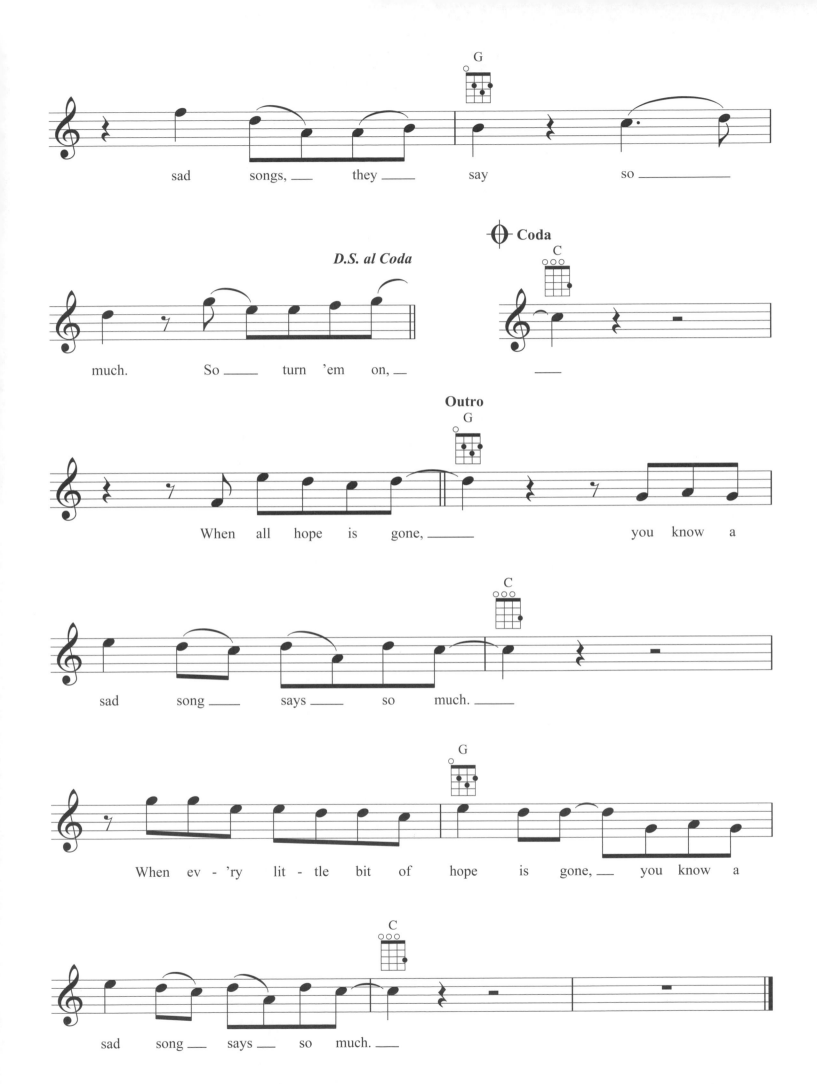

sad   songs, ___ they ___ say   so _____

D.S. al Coda

⊕ Coda

much.   So ___ turn 'em on, ___   ___

Outro

When all hope is gone, _____   you know a

sad   song ___ says ___ so much. _____

When ev - 'ry lit - tle bit of hope is gone, ___ you know a

sad   song ___ says ___ so much. ___

Shake It Off

Words and Music by Taylor Swift, Max Martin and Shellback

but I can't make 'em stay.
I make the moves up as I go.

At least, that's what people say, _____ mm,
And that's what they don't know, _____ mm,

mm. That's what peo - ple say, _____ mm, mm. But I keep
mm. That's what they don't know, _____ mm, mm. But I keep

Pre-Chorus

cruis - ing; can't stop, won't stop mov - ing. } It's
cruis - ing; can't stop, won't stop groov - ing.

like I got this mu - sic in my mind say - ing,

"It's gon - na be al - right." _____ 'Cause the

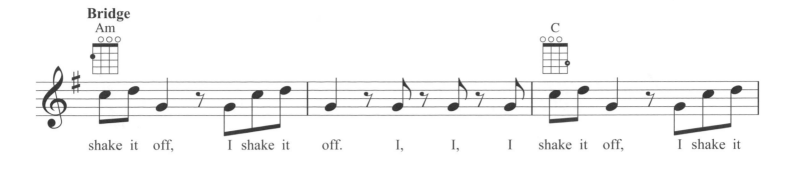

Bridge

shake it off,   I shake it   off.   I,   I,   I   shake it off,   I shake it

off.   I,   I,   I   shake it off,   I shake it   off.   I,   I,   I

shake   it   off,   I shake it   off. _____

(Ooh, _____ ooh!)

Interlude

1. *Spoken: (See additional lyrics)*
2. *Rap: (See additional lyrics)*

D.S. al Coda

Rap ends   Yeah, _____   oh. _____ 'Cause the

off. (Ooh, _____ ooh!) I shake it off, I shake it

off. I, I, I shake it off, I shake it off. I, I, I

shake it off, I shake it off. I, I, I shake it off, I shake it

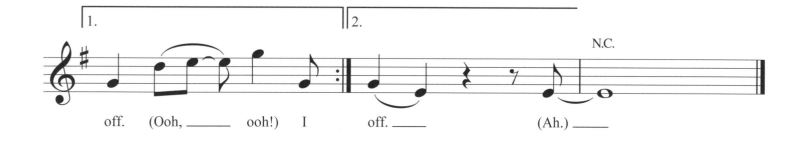

1.
off. (Ooh, _____ ooh!) I

2.
off. _____ (Ah.) _____

Additional Lyrics

Spoken: Hey, hey, hey! Just think: While you've been gettin'
Down and out about the liars and the dirty, dirty cheats of the world,
You could've been gettin' down to this sick beat!

Rap: My ex-man brought his new girlfriend.
She's like, "Oh, my god!" But I'm just gonna shake.
And to the fella over there with the hella good hair,
Won't you come on over, baby? We can shake, shake, shake.

What I Got

Words and Music by Brad Nowell, Eric Wilson, Floyd Gaugh and Lindon Roberts

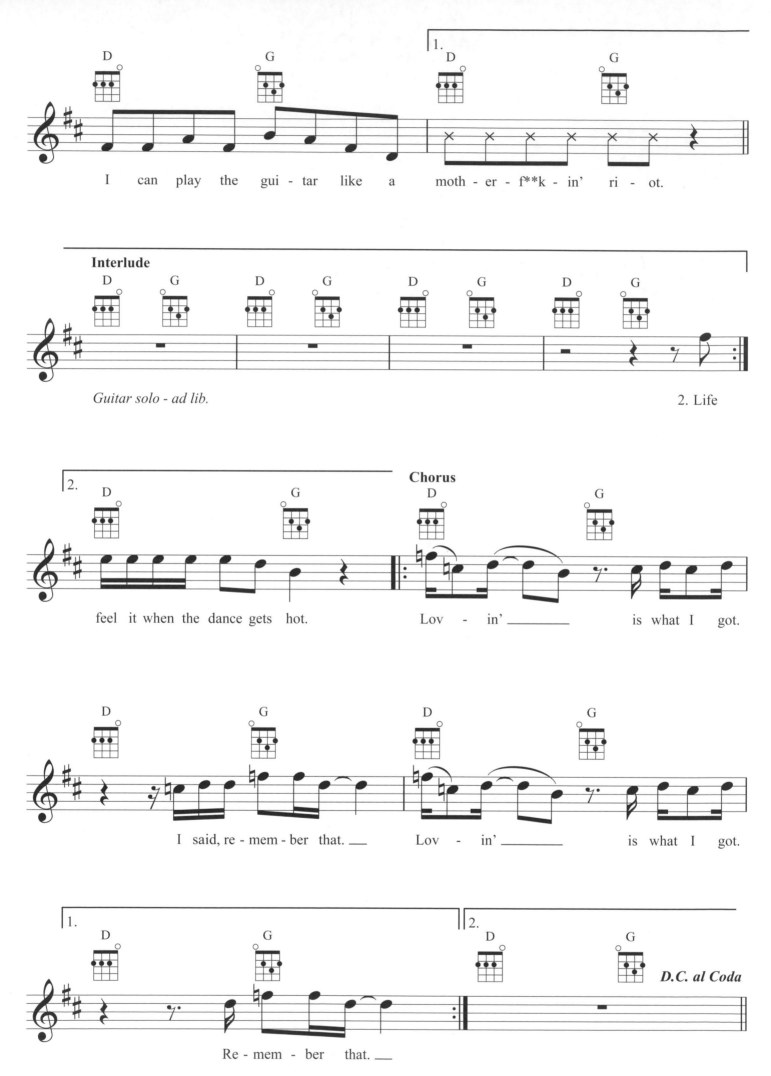

I can play the gui - tar like a moth - er - f**k - in' ri - ot.

Interlude

Guitar solo - ad lib.

2. Life

Chorus

feel it when the dance gets hot.

Lov - in' _____ is what I got.

I said, re - mem - ber that. __

Lov - in' _____ is what I got.

D.C. al Coda

Re - mem - ber that. __

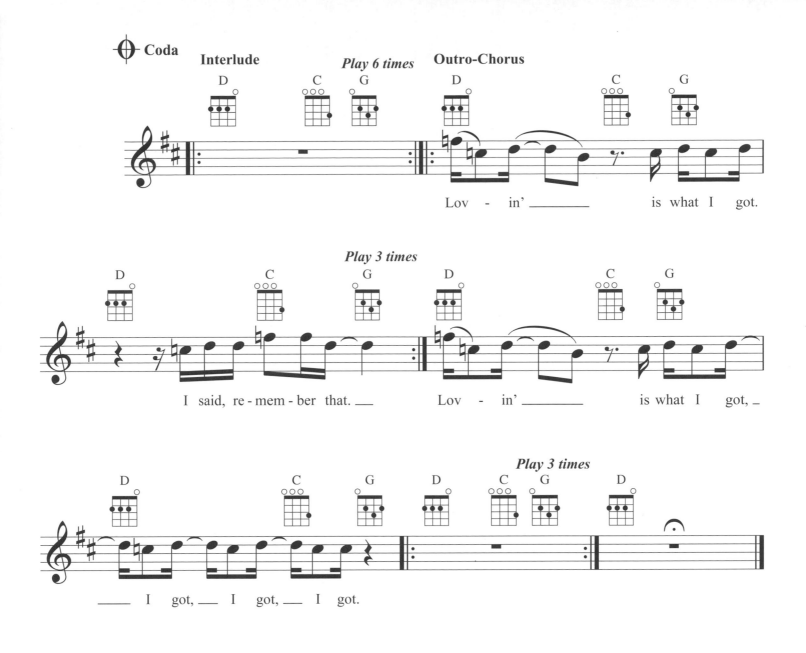

Additional Lyrics

2. Life is (too short), so love the one you got,
   'Cause you might get run over or you might get shot.
   Never start no static, I just get it off my chest.
   Never had to battle with no bulletproof vest.
   Take a small example, take a t-t-t-tip from me:
   Take all of your money, give it all to charity.
   Love is what I got, it's within my reach,
   And the Sublime style's still straight from Long Beach.
   It all comes back to you, you finally get what you deserve.
   Try and test that, you're bound to get served.
   Love's what I got, don't start a riot.
   You'll feel it when the dance gets hot.

3. I don't cry when my dog runs away.
   I don't get angry at the bills I have to pay.
   I don't get angry when my mom smokes pot,
   Hits the bottle and moves right to the rock.
   F**kin' and fightin', it's all the same.
   Livin' with Louie Dog's the only way to stay sane.
   Let the lovin', let the lovin' come back to me. *(To Coda)*

Steal My Kisses

Words and Music by Ben Harper

1. I pulled in to Nash - ville, Ten - nes - see, but you would - n't e - ven come ___ a - round ___ to see me. And since you're head - ing up ___ to Car - o - li - na, you know I'm gon - na be right ___ there ___ be - hind ___ ya. 'Cause I

2., 3. *See additional lyrics*

Chorus

al - ways have __ to steal __ my kiss - es from you.   I

al - ways have __ to steal __ my kiss - es from you.

Al - ways have __ to steal __ my kiss - es from _____ you.   I

al - ways have __ to steal __ my kiss - es from __ you. __   2. Now, I'd __ you.
3. Now,

Additional Lyrics

2. Now, I'd love to feel that warm southern rain.
   Just to hear it fall is the sweetest sounding thing.
   And to see it fall on your simple country dress,
   It's like heaven to me, I must confess.

3. Now, I've been hanging 'round you for days,
   But when I lean in, you just turn your head away.
   Whoa, no, you didn't mean that.
   She said, "I love the way you think, but I hate the way you act."

Used to Love Her

**Words and Music by W. Axl Rose, Slash, Izzy Stradlin',
Duff McKagan and Steven Adler**

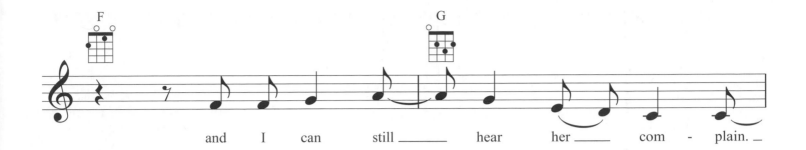

and I can still _____ hear her _____ com - plain. _

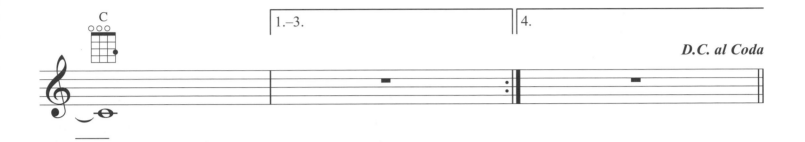

1.–3.   4.

D.C. al Coda

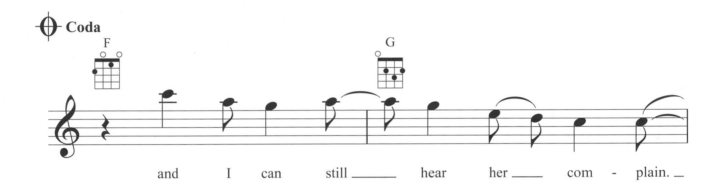

Coda

and I can still _____ hear her _____ com - plain. _

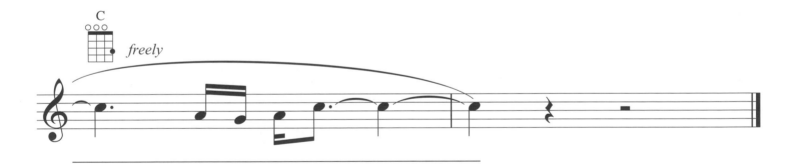

freely

Additional Lyrics

2. I used to love her, but I had to kill her.
   I used to love her, but I had to kill her.
   I knew I'd miss her, so I had to keep her.
   She's buried right in my back yard.

3. I used to love her, but I had to kill her.
   I used to love her, but I had to kill her.
   She bitched so much she drove me nuts,
   And now we're happier this way.

UKULELE CHORD SONGBOOKS

This series features convenient 6" x 9" books with complete lyrics and chord symbols for dozens of great songs. Each song also includes chord grids at the top of every page and the first notes of the melody for easy reference.

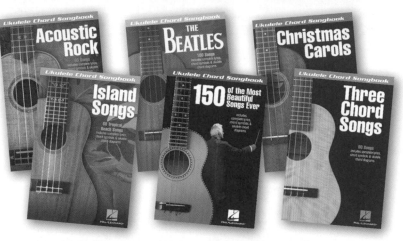

ACOUSTIC ROCK

60 tunes: American Pie • Band on the Run • Catch the Wind • Daydream • Every Rose Has Its Thorn • Hallelujah • Iris • More Than Words • Patience • The Sound of Silence • Space Oddity • Sweet Talkin' Woman • Wake up Little Susie • Who'll Stop the Rain • and more.
00702482 . . . . $15.99

THE BEATLES

100 favorites: Across the Universe • Carry That Weight • Dear Prudence • Good Day Sunshine • Here Comes the Sun • If I Fell • Love Me Do • Michelle • Ob-La-Di, Ob-La-Da • Revolution • Something • Ticket to Ride • We Can Work It Out • and many more.
00703065 . . . . $19.99

BEST SONGS EVER

70 songs: All I Ask of You • Bewitched • Edelweiss • Just the Way You Are • Let It Be • Memory • Moon River • Over the Rainbow • Someone to Watch over Me • Unchained Melody • You Are the Sunshine of My Life • You Raise Me Up • and more.
00117050 . . . . $16.99

CHILDREN'S SONGS

80 classics: Alphabet Song • "C" Is for Cookie • Do-Re-Mi • I'm Popeye the Sailor Man • Mickey Mouse March • Oh! Susanna • Polly Wolly Doodle • Puff the Magic Dragon • The Rainbow Connection • Sing • Three Little Fishies (Itty Bitty Poo) • and many more.
00702473 . . . . $14.99

CHRISTMAS CAROLS

75 favorites: Away in a Manger • Coventry Carol • The First Noel • Good King Wenceslas • Hark! the Herald Angels Sing • I Saw Three Ships • Joy to the World • O Little Town of Bethlehem • Still, Still, Still • Up on the Housetop • What Child Is This? • and more.
00702474 . . . . $14.99

CHRISTMAS SONGS

55 Christmas classics: Do They Know It's Christmas? • Frosty the Snow Man • Happy Xmas (War Is Over) • Jingle-Bell Rock • Little Saint Nick • The Most Wonderful Time of the Year • White Christmas • and more.
00101776 . . . . $14.99

ISLAND SONGS

60 beach party tunes: Blue Hawaii • Day-O (The Banana Boat Song) • Don't Worry, Be Happy • Island Girl • Kokomo • Lovely Hula Girl • Mele Kalikimaka • Red, Red Wine • Surfer Girl • Tiny Bubbles • Ukulele Lady • and many more.
00702471 . . . . $16.99

150 OF THE MOST BEAUTIFUL SONGS EVER

150 melodies: Always • Bewitched • Candle in the Wind • Endless Love • In the Still of the Night • Just the Way You Are • Memory • The Nearness of You • People • The Rainbow Connection • Smile • Unchained Melody • What a Wonderful World • Yesterday • and more.
00117051 . . . . $24.99

PETER, PAUL & MARY

Over 40 songs: And When I Die • Blowin' in the Wind • Goodnight, Irene • If I Had a Hammer (The Hammer Song) • Leaving on a Jet Plane • Puff the Magic Dragon • This Land Is Your Land • We Shall Overcome • Where Have All the Flowers Gone? • and more.
00121822 . . . . $12.99

THREE CHORD SONGS

60 songs: Bad Case of Loving You • Bang a Gong (Get It On) • Blue Suede Shoes • Cecilia • Get Back • Hound Dog • Kiss • Me and Bobby McGee • Not Fade Away • Rock This Town • Sweet Home Chicago • Twist and Shout • You Are My Sunshine • and more.
00702483 . . . . $14.99

TOP HITS

31 hits: The A Team • Born This Way • Forget You • Ho Hey • Jar of Hearts • Little Talks • Need You Now • Rolling in the Deep • Teenage Dream • Titanium • We Are Never Ever Getting Back Together • and more.
00115929 . . . . $14.99

Prices, contents, and availability subject to change without notice.

www.halleonard.com